M000160091

# SCHIRMER'S LIBRARY
## OF MUSICAL CLASSICS

Vol. 2117

# Three Romantic Violin Concertos

## Bruch, Mendelssohn, Tchaikovsky

### For Violin and Piano

ISBN 978-1-4950-1042-2

## G. SCHIRMER, *Inc.*

DISTRIBUTED BY

HAL•LEONARD®
CORPORATION

7777 W. BLUEMOUND RD. P.O. BOX 13819 MILWAUKEE, WI 53213

Copyright © 2015 by G. Schirmer, Inc. (ASCAP) New York, NY
International Copyright Secured. All Rights Reserved.
**Warning: Unauthorized reproduction of this publication is
prohibited by Federal law and subject to criminal prosecution.**

www.musicsalesclassical.com
www.halleonard.com

# CONTENTS

# Concerto
## for Violin in G minor, Op. 26

### I. Prelude

Max Bruch

Edited and fingered by
Henry Schradieck

Copyright © 1900 by G. Schirmer, (Inc.)
Copyright renewal assigned, 1928, to G. Schirmer (Inc.)

attacca

# II. Adagio

18

## III. Finale

# Concerto
## for Violin in E minor, Op. 64

Edited and fingered by
Henry Schradieck

Felix Mendelssohn

49

# Concerto
## for Violin in D Major, Op. 35

Edited and fingered by
Philipp Mittell

Pyotr Il'Yich Tchaikovsky

Copyright © 1918 by G. Schirmer, Inc.

66

72

# Canzonetta

94